THE AFRICAN SUN

Collected Poems by

Michael Sheridan Stone

i

Imprimata

Published by **Imprimata**

A CIP Catalogue record for this book is available
from the British Library

ISBN 978-1-906192-32-7

Set in Warnock Pro with InDCS4

Printed in Great Britain

Cover photograph by John de Kock, *in memoriam*

Imprimata

Imprimata Publishers Limited
50 Albemarle Street, London W1S 4BD.

To Africa - its landscape, wildlife
and, above all, its people.

— and, also :

To Ann,

In appreciation of your
generous remarks about
my poems at Kenwood
House and in the hope
that you will enjoy his
wider collection.

With best wishes,

Michael Stone

St. John's Wood,
1st April, 2010

Acknowledgements

As I state in the Foreword, the poems in the book were written to satisfy personal needs and were not intended for publication. That they are now being published is due largely to the encouragement or exhortation of a number of friends, including Arthur, Helen, Margie, Wendy, David, Maeve and Nanika. My thanks are gratefully conveyed to you all and also to Lulu for her assistance with the final preparation of the manuscript.

Contents

Foreword

I cannot legitimately call myself a poet. I merely have intermittent poetic impulses that are triggered by episodes and emotions, primarily involving Africa. Although I have lived most of my life in England, I am African in heart, spirit, temperament and voice and each year I try to spend time somewhere on the continent. Unhappily my travels no longer encompass my former homeland of Zimbabwe, to which I have no intention of returning until the forces of evil that now dominate and destroy it are spent. But it is forever in my thoughts and much of my poetry has a Zimbabwean theme. Once it was wistful but it has become increasingly pained and angry.

My poetic output is scant and was never intended for publication. I have written my poems to satisfy particular needs of my own and, because they are so personal, I have exposed them to very few people. They have been kind enough to encourage me to share them with a wider audience and this I am doing, albeit with a strong measure of reticence. How can I expect outsiders to relate to my worship of the African sun and the African bush or the joy of my encounters with elephants, leopards, flufftails and snakes or my deep affection for the African people or my implacable opposition to the tyrants who are blighting their lives? I have provided some notes to explain the context or tone of certain poems, or words or expressions in them, but I appreciate that, at least in part, they may remain somewhat opaque or elusive to those without African affiliations.

The poems are divided by geography and, within those divisions, are placed in some sort of chronological order. This does not necessarily indicate when the poems were written, merely when the events that inspired them occurred (or were imagined). In the case of 'The African Sun', there were twin inspirations, the first in 1981, when I began the poem, and the second in 2006, when I 'completed' it – before the several revisions it has undergone since!

I hope that something in the poems will strike a chord with you.

Michael Sheridan Stone
London, April 2009

ZIMBABWEAN POEMS

Introduction

I spent all of my formative years in Rhodesia (as Zimbabwe then was) and, despite not having lived there for all of four decades, it still claims a special place in my heart – although that heart is now deeply pained by the country's desperate plight. It is beyond comprehension how a nation which, as little as ten to fifteen years ago, was held out as a shining example within Africa of prosperity, stability and high educational, health and social standards, should have been catapulted into ruin so rapidly and, it would seem, so irreversibly. While the vast majority of a once proud population live in utter destitution, without access to food, clean water, sanitation, medical treatment, schools or employment, and the Zimbabwe dollar has lost value at a rate previously unimagined by mankind, the ruling elite pays no heed and continues to flourish on what little remains of the fat of the land.

I am both saddened and angered beyond measure at the situation and the seeming inviolability of President Robert Mugabe and his henchmen, because I have yet to meet any finer person than the typical Zimbabwean, whether he or she be Mashona or Matabele. The poems in the second half of this section of the book reflect not only my own despair but also, far more importantly, that of people who have known incomparably better days which neither they nor their children nor, most probably, their grandchildren, will ever again experience.

I will return to the poems in question after retracing my steps to happier times in Zimbabwe. In 1966 I was fortunate enough to obtain a Rhodes Scholarship to study at Oxford University and left Rhodesia for what turned out to be the final time the following year. When I eventually went back to Salisbury (soon to be Harare) on business in April 1980, the country had been transformed into the newly independent Zimbabwe, with a government of national unity blessed with multiple talents, and tourists were flocking back to the Victoria Falls, game reserves and eastern highland resorts. I had missed thirteen years of UDI (Unilateral Declaration of Independence) and the concomitant international isolation, sanctions and 'war of liberation'.

I became reacquainted with close friends from school, enjoyed the delights of the bush and generally felt I had returned home. But not having shared the pain of the period of strife and armed struggle with my former countrymen, I quickly realised that I did not truly 'belong' and my poem 'Home' records that stark realization, as does 'The African Sun' in a gentler and more whimsical way. 'A Soldier' was triggered by the sight of a man in combat dress trudging morosely through the streets of the capital; he too was an outsider in this new society. The sonnet 'The Search' is a lament for my failure to 'communicate' with my late brother David when I visited his final resting place in the Warren Hills; he died tragically young in 1964. 'First Love' and 'The Peregrine' are in a much lighter vein, as are 'The Silence of the Veldt' and the three poems comprising the Elephants trilogy, although the adventures they describe occurred several years later, between 1985 and 1992; some supplementary notes on them are contained in the Appendix.

These were idyllic times, not just for me but also for a good proportion of Zimbabweans, with the wielders of power being generally benevolent despite showing increasingly despotic tendencies. The dark happenings in Matabeleland in the early 1980s were brushed under the carpet although the Matabele themselves have never forgotten or forgiven them - and never will. 'The Angry Child' provides a harrowing account of the atrocities visited upon innocent people. I would recommend that you read the detailed notes in the Appendix before tackling the poem itself as this will lend clarity to the events and emotions it describes. Even in 1980, as recorded in the ditty 'Comradeship', I had detected cracks in the relationship between Mashona and Matabele.

When I last visited Zimbabwe in October 1998 the country remained a wonderful place for a holiday but the infrastructure was definitely creaking. A few years later commercial farms were invaded by so-called 'war veterans', laid to waste and rendered totally unproductive. The economy went into steep decline, the key utilities and services crumbled, there were enhanced levels of oppression and corruption, and the quality of life, for all but a privileged few, plummeted to unbelievable depths. The African dream had become a nightmare, as I relate in 'The Distant Drums'.

I have watched the unfolding tragedy from afar, my knowledge of the situation being gleaned from clandestine television reports and, most recently, discussion with the young Zimbabwean participants at the leadership programmes run by the African Leadership Institute, about which more can be learned from my supplementary notes on 'Regeneration' on page 97. One such discussion, with a doctor from Harare, resulted in 'The Doctor's Dilemma'. Television pictures led to 'Emptiness', 'Barbed Wire' and 'The Birthday Party'. Watching a would-be refugee clambering exhaustedly beneath barbed wire at the border with South Africa near Beit Bridge (where

President Mugabe celebrated his 84th birthday a short while afterwards) was deeply moving and left me hoping that he would discover a better future in the wealthier neighbour to the south – but recent history suggests that this is unlikely to be the case.

Let us hope that the sorely tested spirit of 'Ubuntu' will ultimately prevail within all ranks of Zimbabwean society. More about this uplifting African philosophy can be found in the poem by that name and in the supplementary notes on pages 95 and 96. Otherwise the spectre of 'Closure' draws ever closer in my cherished former homeland.

The African Sun

Once I owned a blood red ball
And tossed it high above the hill,
I watched it deftly fall to earth,
And scamper round of its free will.

Above each crest it peeped and winked
And bounded left and chortled right,
It pranced until the darkness came,
Then slithered quickly from my sight.

Each new morning up it rose,
And teased me as I came to play,
It bobbed beyond my stretching arms
And melted gently into day.

It lost all hint of shape and bounce
And vanished in amorphous blue;
Then snubbed me as I strained my eye
To heaven where the eagles flew.

It reappeared late afternoon
And greeted me upon my lawn,
Ducked within my boyish clasp,
And so another game was born.

We played that game for many years,
'Til I grew tired of childish joy,
I closed my mind to lighter whims,
And cast aside my lifelong toy.

I moved afar to sullen climes
Where sun was lost to cloud and rain,
And now that I was growing old
I yearned to find my friend again.

So back I went to Africa,
And gazed intent at cloudless sky,
I watched the sun from dawn to dusk,
Creeping low and perching high;
But though I earned some inner peace,
I found whatever ploy I'd try
Could not unleash that long lost ball,
Lodged firmly in a childhood eye.

FIRST LOVE

I sat above a river bank
And scoured the bush around,
Searching for some creatures
To make my young heart pound.

I watched hyena grin and lope,
Some buck and warthog too,
But all of them flew out of mind
The moment I saw you.

You lounged below me on a rock,
Lit by the morning sun,
Your beauty took my breath away,
I begged you not to run.

You wore a finely tailored coat
That stretched from head to paw,
Coloured cream with dark black spots
No human hand could draw.

I looked into your amber eyes,
They stared intently back,
You had a regal quality
That other females lack.

Your sharp white teeth flashed me a smile,
You growled some sounds of bliss,
I hankered to get close to you
But feared your deadly kiss.

Then you rose and walked at pace
Beside the sunlit stream,
I waved my hand in sad farewell
And saw your whiskers gleam.

You gazed at me one final time,
Then left me there above,
I never have forgotten you,
You[1] were my first true love.

---

1 *For those who have not yet guessed, the subject of the poem is a leopard!*

HOME

My dry lips touched the grass of home,
Kissed in joy the sunburnt earth,
Whispered heartfelt words of love
To the land that gave me birth.

I lay at peace in timeless sun,
Gifting warmth from clear blue sky,
Embraced the hills I knew so well,
The little stream that trickled by.

My mind leapt back to carefree youth,
Rued the lost years spent away -
Not half the years Time stole from men
Whose lives were taken in this vlei[1].

Could that cheeky go-away bird[2],
Chiding me for creeping near,
Once have scolded combatants,
Seeking refuge from their fear?

Did this stately mukwa[3] tree,
Blessed with magic healing charms,
Cling more tightly to its bark
And shelter strident men at arms?

Did this quietly rustling wind,
Weaving gently through my hair,
Wail and roar and snarl in hate
As slaughter laid the bushveld bare?

Had the auburn grass sprung tall,
Nourished by the unclaimed dead?
Was it some old schoolfriend's blood
That stained the sad msasas[4] red?

What gave the country its allure?
- The sacrifice[5] I never shared;
This land belonged to those who fought,
Not to one whom fortune spared.

---

1 *Marshy land*

2 *Grey lourie, whose strident call resembles "Go away!"*

3 *A species of teak; its bark and roots are used in traditional medicine to treat a wide variety of ailments, ranging from malaria to asthma*

4 *A small shapely tree whose leaves have a distinctive amber and wine red colour when they sprout during spring*

5 *Although the precise number of lives lost during the 'war of liberation' in Zimbabwe will never be known, it has been estimated that up to 30,000 people of all races were killed, including several of my school friends and teachers*

A Soldier

I saw a man in battledress today.
His uniform was patterned
In green and brown and grey;
He was indeed a striking sight,
More coloured than a jay;
Tall and broad, erect and strong,
I yearned to shout "hooray!";
I saw a man in battledress today.

I saw a man in battledress today.
He should have been a young man,
Aged twenty years, I'd say,
But ceaseless war had stricken him
And dredged his youth away;
His well-tanned face was haggard -
He'd little time for play;
I saw a man in battledress today.

I saw a man in battledress today.
The surgeon's skill had salvaged him
To kill and earn his pay;
His reknit arm was sound enough
To fight on, come what may;
But no doctor's hand could heal the wound
To a soul in disarray;
I saw a man in battledress today.

I saw a man in battledress today.
Exhausted now by conflict,
His mind began to stray
To the pleasures of his childhood,
When he felt no urge to slay,
And his mother's shouted orders
Were so easy to obey;
I saw a man in battledress today.

I saw a man in battledress today.
The enemy was close to him
In search of further prey,
And the greater foe within himself
Lent torment to dismay;
Then I put aside the mirror
And ushered care away;
I died a man in battledress today.

THE PEREGRINE

Suddenly I broke away and lived;
My soul touched sky
And soared untrammelled
To the beckoning sun.

I sped alone beyond the earth,
Remote from man's gaunt bond,
And, spreading wing, exalted
In the joy of silent poise.

My perfect pitch awakened
Fresh knowledge of myself;
I gloried in the cadence
Of unremitting flight.

Then I saw a doleful dove,
Who had no sense of doom above;
Down I plunged
And stooped and lunged.

I ripped and tore
With beak and claw,
Immersed myself in flesh and gore,
Feasting high but wanting more.

The bird's sweet essence entered me,
Infusing me with love,
My transient day flushed crimson
In homage to the dove.

I hovered softly in repose,
Then drifting idly back to ground,
Sought the gloved hand;
And, thus embraced, I died.

THE SEARCH

I stood alone with you and other
Distant shades, outside my earthly ken,
Yet claiming you as brother,
And sought for you down Time's dark glen,
Past memory of later joy and pain,
To long forgotten days when we were young;
I urged you to appear – in vain,
For I could not use celestial tongue
Or find a wraith with your brief imprint;
No power in me could draw you back
To my vexed mind; the only hint
Of you the staid bronze plaque
Which simply states your name and age,
And when you sped this mortal stage.

COMRADESHIP

How can you be my brother
When you are not like me?
I'm from here, you're from there;
We think quite differently.

We cannot march together;
It is futile to pretend
That I will call you comrade,
For you are not my friend.

The Silence of the Veldt

Creeping out at first light,
A clamour in my ear,
Birds of all descriptions
Singing loud and clear,
I marvel at the joyous din
That greets the break of day;
Young impala prance about
And infant warthogs play.
Then noise is cruelly shattered,
A creature's doom is spelt,
There's the sound of utter silence -
The silence of the veldt.

Melting in the harsh sun,
My nerves severely frayed,
Animals now well dispersed
In search of scanty shade,
I stagger blindly through the bush
To flop down on the ground;
The cloying heat saps energy
And blankets out all sound.
Oppression takes a stifling grip
That tightens like a belt;
I touch a wall of silence -
The silence of the veldt.

Crouching at a waterhole
Towards the end of day,
Creatures taking final drinks
Before they slip away,
I smell deep fear in animals
Who may not live for long,
The stench of rotting carcases

Is suffocating song.
The grassland reeks of pungent dung
Where buffalo have dwelt;
These odours seal the silence -
The silence of the veldt.

Sprawled beside a camp fire,
A Castle[1] in my hand,
The birds no longer singing
And peace across the land,
I wonder why this is the time
When beers are at their best,
Even though they're warm and flat
And lack their usual zest.
It's not the content of the brew
That makes my taste buds melt,
But the flavour of the silence -
The silence of the veldt.

Sleeping by a bush trail
Where albidas[2] abound,
My colleagues snoring gently,
No other hint of sound,
I sense the spectre of a beast
Steal near with ghostly tread;
An elephant is chewing pods
Ten metres from my head.
My eyes reveal it standing there
As quiet as if it knelt;
It symbolises silence -
The silence of the veldt.

---

1 *A leading brand of beer in southern Africa*

2 *A species of acacia tree, the fruits/pods of which are an important component of the diets of large antelope, buffalo and elephant*

ELEPHANTS*

Have you played with elephants?
If not, you've missed some fun;
Settle gently in your chair,
I'll tell you how it's done;
Choose a smart camp on a hill,
Remote in Hwange Park[1],
Stroll around the bush all day,
Then wander back at dark;
Light a fire to have a braai[2],
Open up cold beers,
Let the moonlight wash your face
And rinse away your fears;
Prepare to hear the tallest tales,
Then tell some of your own,
Why honey badgers[3] strike the groin,
How loud their victims moan;
Have another beer or two,
Eat some wors[4] and steak,
Stretch out on the luscious grass,
Give your mind a break.

Lift your eyes in wonderment
As elephants trudge in,
Past the braai and past yourself,
Ten metres from your chin;
You never hear them on the move,
They walk as if on foam,
Emerging from the distant bush
To this, their second home;
They drink from leaky water pipes
That make the grass grow green,
They mill around, ignoring you,
Though you've been clearly seen;
You want to take some backward steps,

But you are held transfixed,
Mighty beasts loll everywhere,
Bulls and youths all mixed;
Tusks are flashing near your fire,
Trunks are intertwined,
The elephants are playing games
With any toys they find.

You decide you're not a toy,
Resolve to rest your head,
But there are eighteen elephants
Between you and your bed;
They show no sign of bowing out,
So what are you to do?
Take a further beer in hand,
It's time to think things through;
Stride towards the animals
That block your bed-bound path,
Ask them please to step aside,
Almost hear them laugh;
Raise your voice a notch or two,
Holler in their ear,
Clank beer cans incessantly,
Push them in the rear;
Gentle giants dance aside,
Let you through their ranks,
You have played with elephants,
For which give hearty thanks.

* Supplementary notes on this poem can be found in the Appendix

1 *A game reserve in the western part of Zimbabwe quite close to the Victoria Falls*

2 *Barbecue*

3 *Also known as the ratel. It is similar in size and shape to the European badger and is widely regarded as the fiercest animal in the African bush*

4 *Boerewors, a traditional South African sausage, that tastes best when barbecued and eaten outside*

MORE ELEPHANTS*

Have you slept with elephants?
I have, but just with one;
Listen to me for a while,
I'll tell you how it's done;
Take the hottest day you've known,
Start a gruelling trek[1],
Strip off all the clothes you donned,
Tie them round your neck;
Sweat your way along a gorge,
Bathe in every pool,
Cling to any scrap of shade,
Keep your forehead cool;
Plaster on the tanning oil,
Feel your bare skin bake,
Watch klipspringer[2] bound uphill,
Dodge the odd sand snake;
Then at last your due reward,
Taitas[3] flying free,
Speeding low across the cliffs,
The rarest birds you'll see.

Elated by the taitas' flight,
Tramp back down the trail,
Time to choose a spot to sleep
Away from rock and shale;
Clamber stiffly up a slope,
Pant from constant thirst,
Gasp for breath each step you take,
Think your lungs must burst;
Halfway up the endless hill,
Find a spacious cave,
Vaulted roof and sandy floor,
The refuge that you crave;
Start to move your clobber[4] in,

Hear the whine of bees,
Hurl yourself below the swarm,
Crawl out on your knees;
On and upwards still you go,
Then you strike the top,
Reach a glade of albidas[5],
Decide that's where you'll stop.

Relax at last as darkness falls,
Light your small gas hob,
Cook your meat and beans and pap[6],
Mealies[7] on the cob;
Rest your weary, aching limbs,
Free your mind from doubt,
Put your Qantas eyeshades[8] on,
Block the moonlight out;
Sink into untroubled sleep,
Then hear a crackling sound,
Gently ease your eyeshades off
To see what's on the ground;
An elephant is sidling close,
As quietly as can be,
Intent on chewing tasty pods
He's stripping off a tree;
The animal has come in peace,
So shut your eyes and snore,
You have slept with elephant(s);
How can you ask for more?

---

* *Supplementary notes on this poem can be found in the Appendix*

1 *A long arduous journey, in this case on foot*

2 *An extremely agile small antelope*

3 *Taita falcons, which are among Africa's rarest and most elusive birds*

4 *Clothing and personal items*

5 *A species of acacia tree, the fruits/pods of which are an important component of the diets of large antelope, buffalo and elephant*

6 *A solid maize meal paste, rather like white polenta*

7 *Maize or corn*

8 *These were a particularly villainous shade of red!*

ELEPHANTS AGAIN*

Have you swum with elephants?
I nearly did, my son;
If you want to follow me,
I'll tell you how it's done;
Make your way to Mana Pools[1],
Burned russet by the drought,
Trample through the arid bush,
Throw inhibition out;
Fetch a trusted old canoe,
Start your trip downstream,
Trail a line behind the boat,
Try to catch some bream;
Sink a beer Zimbabwe style,
Tilt your head and pour,
Kick your legs until it's drained,
Then go back for more;
Chew some biltong[2] or droewors[3],
Get your salt intake,
Paddle harder for a while,
Earn a short smoke break.

Prepare to face some further pain,
Oil yourself and fry,
Hippos lurk among the reeds
But let you safely by;
Join up with the other boats,
Legs will lock them tight,
Time means nothing in the bush,
Drift for your delight;
Jacanas[4] trot on lily leaves,
Carmines[5] dart from banks,
Cheer as stately saddlebills[6]
Dominate greenshanks[7];
Shake off all your lethargy,

Row at breakneck pace,
Steer at every stump and arch,
Win each hard fought race;
Hit a basking crocodile,
Feel it lift your boat,
Pray to all the river gods,
Come back down afloat.

Stop beneath a sloping bank,
Shed your shirt and shoes,
Climb into a sandy cove,
Sluice the soiled canoes;
Zambezi glimmers in the sun,
Mana's to the fore,
Fill your lungs with Africa,
Knock at heaven's door;
Elephants arrive unheard,
Five big bulls plod down,
Spray themselves with cooling mud,
Start to play the clown;
Find yourself five yards from them,
Mark their every sound,
Sidle back a foot or two,
Turn the boats around;
Jumbos now decide to drink,
Time to move away;
You've almost swum with elephants,
That's surely made your day.

1 A magical game reserve adjoining the Zambezi River below Lake Kariba in Zimbabwe

2 Strips of dried venison or beef

3 Dried sausage

4 A small elegant wading bird; unusually, the male rears the young

5 Carmine bee-eaters

6 Saddlebill storks, the largest riverine birds at Mana Pools

7 Medium size wading birds that are also found throughout Europe

THE ANGRY CHILD*

"Let me tell you of our triumph",
Said the master to the school,
"In the ten short years of freedom
That we've gloried in black rule.
Great unity of purpose
Has brought us wealth and peace,
An undivided nation
Fit to rival ancient Greece;
A government of talent,
With broad ethnicity,
Humane and democratic,
Representing you and me."

Up jumped a boy of seventeen,
Star pupil of his class,
"I hate to contradict you
But you're talking through your arse.
Where was the single nation
In 1984,
When murderous Mashonas[1]
Lashed my mother red and raw?
Thugs drove up in furtive trucks,
Armed with gun and knife,
Intent on decimation
Of Matabele[2] life.

The truth must now be spoken,
I won't be meek and mild,
I'll tell things as I know them,
I am an angry child."

The master was a kind man
And spoke with sympathy,

"I'm sorry for your mother,
But I think you should agree
That minor local problems
Occur in every land,
And even in Zimbabwe
Some men get out of hand.
There were a lot of dissidents
Who needed tight control,
But their treatment was quite gentle
By a disciplined patrol."

The schoolboy's voice rose up again,
"You can't believe all this,
I want to be respectful
But you're full of wind and piss.
How disciplined were soldiers
Who burst into our hut
And mauled and raped my sister
Like a Matabele slut?
They marauded through my country,
Bulawayo to World's View[3],
Threw bombs at homes and churches,
Near Malindidzimu[4].

The truth must now be spoken
Evasion makes me wild,
The time for tact is over,
I am an angry child."

The master now was somewhat vexed
But tried to stay quite calm,
"It was tragic for your sister
That those men did her some harm;
Their presence there was needed
To supplement the police
In halting Lookout's[5] gangsters

Causing breaches of the peace.
The force they used was proper
To rid the land of scum,
It was only propagandists
Who saw a nightmare come."

The boy sprang up in outrage,
His eyes were fiercely lit,
"You are my trusted teacher
But you're talking utter shit.
My father was no gangster
But he is surely dead,
Those bandits of Mugabe
Drove nails right through his head.
Was it propaganda
That dreamt up Belaghwe[6] ,
Where countless men were butchered
In this country of the free?
The bodies dumped in mineshafts
Have rotted to manure,
But they were Matabele
So it has a golden core.

We can't ignore what happened,
Reports should now be filed,
Until the truth is spoken
I'll be an angry child."

* Supplementary notes on this poem can be found in the Appendix

1 The majority ethnic group in Zimbabwe

2 The minority ethnic group in Zimbabwe

3 A vantage point in the Matopos hills near Bulawayo that was loved by Cecil Rhodes and where he was finally laid to rest

4 Scene of some of the worst atrocities in Matabeleland

5 Lookout Masuku, a leading Matabele activist

6 A brutal detention centre where countless people were tortured and murdered

The Distant Drums

There was a time of dread and fear,
When man went out with gun or spear
To right the wrongs of yesteryear,
In Africa[1].

The battles raged a long, long time,
With streams to cross and hills to climb,
And men sank deep in gore and grime,
In Africa.

And in the distance harsh drums beat
A ruthless rhythm for bare feet.

Countless people died in pain,
Black and white among the slain;
When would peace break out again,
In Africa?

Then at last an end to strife,
With prospects of more normal life,
Surviving men could take a wife,
In Africa.

And in the distance proud drums beat
A rousing rhythm for quick feet.

The wasted years left much to do,
A new regime would see things through,
This was what it promised you,
In Africa.

All the kids were now at school,
A tribute to emergent rule,
This land would be the shining jewel,
Of Africa.

And in the distance soft drums beat
A gentle rhythm for shod feet.

The leaders rode in smart new cars,
Drank their tea from cups, not jars,
They might as well have lived on Mars,
Not Africa.

They lost their focus due to greed
And quite forgot the people's need
To build more homes and plant more seed,
In Africa.

And in the distance sad drums beat
A forlorn rhythm for tired feet.

The people grew extremely poor,
No work on farms or factory floor,
With AIDS a scourge for ever more,
In Africa.

Flimsy shacks were bulldozed down[2]
By soldiers paid to cleanse the town
Of human filth of no renown,
In Africa.

The people had no more to give,
Few mealie[3] cobs were left to sieve,
They've almost lost the will to live,
In Africa.

And now the distant drums were stilled
As all grand hopes and dreams were killed,
In Africa.

---

1 *Specifically Zimbabwe, although the history described will have echoes in other African countries*

2 *A well publicized ruthless episode that was designed to destabilize opponents of President Robert Mugabe*

3 *Maize or corn*

THE DOCTOR'S DILEMMA*

I am a humble doctor
Who has the power to kill,
Not because I want to
Or due to lack of skill.
My power rests in some tablets,
Of which I have but eight,
Each one can help a person
Delay a deadly fate.
There are scores and scores of patients
Who'd like the chance to live,
All of them deserve this,
It's something I can't give.
I can only treat five people,
For a reason I'll explain,
And how I choose that handful
Will cause me heartfelt pain.

Should I give a tablet
To this old man or this youth?
The former aged just twenty eight
If you must know the truth.
No one in Zimbabwe
Survives for long these days;
Adulthood is very brief[1]
For everyone who stays.
Why waste a tablet on a man
Whose life is all but done?
At least he had some pleasant days
Whereas the youth had none.
Will my pill give succour
To a boy as weak as this?
I'll let him have it anyway
And watch him smile in bliss.

Now for tablet number two,
I'll play this by the book,
The candidates are in my room,
A vagrant and a cook.
My choice would seem quite simple,
The cook must win the day,
But often in Zimbabwe
We take the perverse way.
For most of us are vagrants
In this land where few men work,
A tribute to our harsh regime
That deems a job a perk.
The vagrant was a lawyer once,
A man of high renown,
I'll give him my small tablet,
The cook will be let down.

I take another pill in hand
And call the next two in;
A pauper and a millionaire,
One fat, the other thin.
The fat one is the pauper,
Suffering from bloat,
The millionaire is very gaunt
And wears a tatty coat.
It is only in Zimbabwe
That millionaires are poor[2],
They have enough to buy some bread
But very little more.
Their dollars cannot purchase health
Or lasting remedy,
That is why I'll give this man
My tablet number three.

We now reach tablet number four
And two more men arrive,
A Matabele[3] in decline,
Mashona[4] scarce alive.
The latter is my tribesman,
I owe him loyalty,
We grew up in a compound
Where all of us were free.
The nation now is shackled
By Mugabe and his band;
They trample on ambition
And rape this lovely land.
Matabele are our brothers
As we strive for liberty;
This comrade in my wardroom
Will get the pill from me.

One more tablet left to give
And one more man to choose;
Will it be the pious priest,
The thug worse off for booze?
The virtues of the holy man
Shine out for all to see;
The vices of the drunken slob
Have equal clarity.
But he is in the government,
A big noise in this town,
If I don't give him what he wants
He'll close my clinic down.
I want to help the pastor
But he can call on God;
I have to keep my clinic,
So my pill goes to this sod.

Why have I kept three tablets
That many people need?
Is it that I'll sell them,
Provoked by some base greed?
The truth is very simple,
So listen to me, please;
The pills are earmarked for myself -
I have the dread disease.
I could have moved to England
And practised over there,
But stayed to help my people
Through times of great despair.
If I'm to salvage patients,
I must try to stay alive;
Now you know the reason
Why I treated only five.

* Supplementary notes on this poem can be found in the Appendix

1 *The latest figures published by the United Nations record that the life expectancy in Zimbabwe is the lowest in the world, being 37 for men and 34 for women*

2 *When this poem was written, one million Zimbabwe dollars were worth about ten US dollars. Little more than 18 months later, you could substitute 'one trillion' for 'one million'*

3 *A member of the minority ethnic group in Zimbabwe*

4 *A member of the majority ethnic group in Zimbabwe*

*Ubuntu**

What is this thing called *ubuntu*,
Is it a myth or a truth?
Is it the root of our culture,
Or is it a sop to our youth?

Few of us here can explain it
In words we can all understand;
There are myriad meanings to ponder,
Some trite, some impossibly grand.

The version I favour is simple,
Ubuntu is plain 'dignity';
I'm respectful of all other people
And they are respectful of me.

"We only exist in each other",
That's what the traditionalists thirst;
We shouldn't ask more of our comrades
Than we are prepared to do first.

We are those we revere as our forbears
And those who will follow us, too,
We believe in a seamless compassion,
That's why we espouse *ubuntu*.

This concept of interdependence
Is deeply ingrained in us all;
But how can it function in practice
When handfuls make each major call?

The despots who rule us are demons
Who hold all the wealth in their hands,
They care not a jot for their neighbours
And take what they like from their lands.

Our cherished *ubuntu* seems shattered
By those we've entrusted to lead;
They call themselves men of the people
But live by their own selfish creed.

There's no hint of *ubuntu* within them,
Though it's something they loudly proclaim;
They use it to justify pillage
Of community land in their name.

We accept all their words without question
And none of us dare to ask why;
It's "do as I say, not do as I do",
We follow this maxim - or die.

From this you may draw the conclusion
That *ubuntu* is merely deceit,
Power rests in the criminal pagans
With licence to lie and to cheat.

But look in the humbler environs,
You will find that *ubuntu* survives;
There are thousands of acts of devotion
To neighbours with beggarly lives.

There are children who look after orphans
Though they have been orphaned in turn,
There are pastors who challenge oppression
And pray as their small chapels burn.

Some teachers hold firm to tradition
And refuse to invent history,
Some doctors look after poor patients
And decline to accept any fee.

There are honest men still left in business
Who keep their slim workforce afloat;
I'm glad there are one or two policemen
Who afford me the freedom to vote.

If we are to find our salvation
And rebuild our country forthwith,
We must honour this thing called *ubuntu*
And make it a truth, not a myth.

* Supplementary notes on this poem can be found in the Appendix; they include Archbishop Desmond Tutu's pithy explanation of ubuntu

EMPTINESS

I sat in cushioned comfort,
Switched on my TV,
Watched the news with interest,
A film on Zimbabwe;
Some shops I knew were pictured,
But all had empty shelves,
Nothing there for people
To buy to feed themselves;
No milk, no tea, no mealie[1] meal,
No sugar and no meat,
Not a loaf of bread in sight,
No sign of any sweet.

The feature on Zimbabwe
Turned to empty farms,
With no-one left to run them
Save bandits bearing arms;
The fields that grew tobacco
Had largely been destroyed,
The farmers' trusted workers
Were long since unemployed;
No seeds, no plants, no harvest,
No stubble left to burn,
No crops to send to auction,
No export cash to earn.

The news report went further,
Showed the empty schools,
Closed for lack of teachers
Shackled by harsh rules;
Most children had been orphaned
And now were schoolless too,
No adults there to guide them

Or mould their lives anew;
No books, no pens, no writing pads,
No classmates and no games,
No semblance of true childhood,
No dreams or hopes or aims.

We saw the empty shanties,
Reduced to mud and wood,
Bulldozed down by soldiers
Who cleansed this neighbourhood;
The homeless were all jobless,
Crouched begging in the street,
Their spirit now lay broken,
They had no food to eat;
No jobs, no homes, no shelter,
No money and no bread,
No prospects for the future,
They were the living dead.

The final clip of rallies
Made my hackles rise,
Mugabe and his henchmen
Were ranting strings of lies;
No words about the starving,
No-one accepting blame,
No sympathy for people,
No tiny scrap of shame;
No heart, no soul, no conscience,
No guilt and no remorse,
These men of empty vision
Knew no god but force.

---

1 *Maize or corn*

NOSTALGIA

I never venture home these days -
Or where home used to be;
This should come as no surprise
For home was Zimbabwe.

I well remember ideal times,
Not all that long ago[1],
When people sang and joked and laughed,
As happy as they'd know.

The sun shone from a cloudless sky,
Unless we needed rain,
Our fertile land grew fruitful crops,
We stored much surplus grain.

We had the very best hotels,
Fine restaurants by the score,
The tourists flocked to see our land
And came back wanting more.

They travelled to our awesome Falls[2],
True wonder of our age,
Then moved along to Hwange Park[3],
Black rhino[4] held the stage.

Some preferred our eastern hills,
Where trout streams gently flowed,
Vineyards hugged the lower slopes,
Gold wattle[5] fringed the road.

Our schooling made us justly proud,
Set standards that were high,
Instilled in us strong moral codes.
We dared not cheat or lie.

The public figures sought no perks,
They governed for us all,
Inspired a strand of unity
That made us ten feet tall.

Our sportsmen scaled the highest peaks
In integrated teams,
Competing right across the globe,
They matched our wildest dreams.

We'd doctors who could work a cure,
Though very few were ill,
None of us predicted AIDS,
The millions it would kill.

Those who went without a job
Found refuge with their kin,
Ubuntu⁶ spurred the kindest acts,
Support through thick and thin.

Nothing you have read thus far
Reflects the truth today,
Until my home is freshly built,
I'll choose to stay away.

---

1 *The mid 1990s*

2 *The Victoria Falls, one of the seven natural wonders of the modern world*

3 *A magnificent game reserve to the south of Victoria Falls*

4 *The population of black rhino in Zimbabwe in the mid 1980s was the largest in Africa.
The species is now virtually extinct in the country due to unlawful poaching*

5 *A species of acacia tree that has clusters of yellow flowers that remain in bloom for significant
periods of the year*

6 *See poem by that name and the explanatory notes on pages 95 and 96 for further details*

BARBED WIRE

Just twenty miles to Eden[1] now,
Beyond the coiled barbed wire;
Just twenty miles before I eat,
When I'll take refuge from this heat;
Although my body starts to tire,
I must go on somehow.

There'll surely be a richer life
Beyond the coiled barbed wire;
My family fear I won't come back,
But I'll return along this track;
I'll burn again with inner fire,
Have presents for my wife.

Just fifteen miles before I stride
Beyond the coiled barbed wire;
Just fiftèen miles of this sharp pain
That wracks my limbs time and again;
All moisture drained, I can't perspire,
I'll walk until I'm fried.

They tell me only good men rule
Beyond the coiled barbed wire;
Far better than the ones we've got,
Who line their pockets like a shot;
Each one of them a bare-faced liar
Or else an utter fool.

Just ten more miles until I bound
Beyond the coiled barbed wire;
Just ten but I'm a wounded man,
I'll limp along as best I can;
Survival drives my spirit higher,
There's now some firmer ground.

What streams of work might I explore
Beyond the coiled barbed wire?

I was the brightest boy in class,
The hardest tests I'd always pass;
Perhaps my talents will inspire
An office job once more.

Just five short miles then I can burst
Beyond the coiled barbed wire;
Just five but now I pant and wheeze,
I'm crawling on my hands and knees;
I won't collapse, I'll not expire,
I'll reach the border first.

What sort of shelter will I find
Beyond the coiled barbed wire?
A million Shonas[2] went before,
There must be room for just one more;
I know I'll sorely miss my kia[3],
My father who is blind.

I'm crouched and gazing at the land
Beyond the coiled barbed wire;
I try to burrow underneath,
Get ripped and torn but grit my teeth;
Late rescue when my plight looks dire,
A kind and gentle hand.

I wonder how long I will last
Beyond the coiled barbed wire;
I've heard that crime is very high[4],
There's every chance that I will die;
It's too late now, I can't retire,
Zimbabwe's in the past.

---

1 *South Africa, perceived by many Zimbabweans to be the land of plenty and of boundless opportunity*

2 *Mashonas, the largest ethnic group in Zimbabwe*

3 *Home dwelling, often rudimentary*

4 *There is a frightening incidence of violent crime in parts of South Africa, not least in Johannesburg, towards which most Zimbabwean refugees gravitate*

THE BIRTHDAY PARTY*

Cheer more loudly at the back - he's[1] eighty four today;
He wants to hear his people sing,
Expects to feel the heavens ring,
With welling praise and joy;
He says that he's prepared to stay
In power while he's alive,
That means until he's ninety five;
So chant his name more loudly - or you'll regret it, boy.

Don that shirt they've given you - the one that matches his;
It shows his proud and cultured face,
An icon for his Shona race,
That men must hold in thrall;
He shouts and rants with vim and fizz,
His tirade fills the air,
Let men oppose him if they dare;
So wave your arms more fiercely - give that salute your all.

Clap those hands much harder, please - he craves that
    hot applause;
He starts his lavish birthday feast,
They've freshly killed a peasant's beast,
To honour him as god;
There cannot be a better cause
To raid that sealed food store,
A gift by donors to the poor;
So gorge until you vomit - you lucky, greedy sod.

Blow up all those red balloons - they'll soon adorn the sky;
The land around is parched and brown
But he's come here to paint the town
With troops of young war vets[2];
He'll still preside when they all die[3],
Until that time they'll thrive,
His gaunt opponents won't survive;
So roar you'll always love him - lest someone here forgets.

Jeer those dolts behind the wire - the wrong side of Beit Bridge[5];
He's come to prove that he's in charge,
He doesn't feed on bread and marge [5]
Like those sad refugees;
He stands aloof on that high ridge
To mock their feeble taunts,
They'll never share the wealth he flaunts;
So sing out Happy Birthday - and sing more loudly, please.

* *Supplementary notes on this poem can be found in the Appendix*

1 *President Robert Mugabe*

2 *Alleged veterans of the 'war of liberation' in Rhodesia during the 1970s; many of those attending the birthday celebration could not have been born before 1990!*

3 *An allusion to the incredibly low life expectancy in the present-day Zimbabwe*

4 *A town on the Limpopo River on the Zimbabwean side of the border with South Africa. As the Limpopo is mainly dry these days, the border is protected by barbed wire [see previous poem by that name]*

5 *Margarine*

CLOSURE

Turn off your tap, redundant rain,
There's nothing left to grow;
Let drought pervade this stark domain
'Til shoots of justice show.

Blow yourself out, unhelpful wind,
The stench of death can lurk;
Let stillness swamp the men who've sinned
'Til screams of protest work.

Switch off your light, unwelcome sun,
While madmen stalk this land;
Let darkness stay 'til we've begun
To touch bright freedom's hand.

SOUTH AFRICAN POEMS

Introduction

Since January 2003 I have travelled to South Africa at least once per year and have come to know and love the mountain village of Barrydale in the Overberg on the fringes of the Little Karoo. It is a relaxed and tranquil place, mercifully free of the security fences and ferocious dogs that besmirch the more affluent suburbs of South Africa's larger towns. Barrydale is an ideal place to reflect on life, and on your vocation in life, more particularly along one of the less frequented mountain trails that weave their meandering way through the softly coloured fynbos. You may encounter the odd snake (as I recount in 'Interlude'), although they generally slide away when they hear you coming, but this only adds spice to the trek. The greater likelihood – and potential danger – is that you will unwittingly diverge from the trail, as it is all too easy to do, both above Barrydale and in life. At the end of your walk you can relax and reflect at The Country Pumpkin or The Blue Cow or another of the village's delightful tearooms. My own journey of intended self-discovery is described in 'The Pumpkin or the Cow'.

I can thoroughly recommend an excursion to an arid enclave known as The Manger that is a short distance from Barrydale. It is the site of what I believe to be Africa's only Buddhist pagoda. Contiguous to that somewhat incongruous landmark is a beautiful labyrinth fringed by pink flowers and demarcated by low walls of rose quartz crystal. Speak nicely to its owner, Nola Frazer, and she will permit you to enter the labyrinth. Then stroll languidly towards its central 'petals', there to sit in welcome shade, and surrender yourself to passive contemplation. The labyrinth deserves its own poem, which I have yet to write; it certainly inspired me to revive and complete 'The Distant Drums', which is to be found in the Zimbabwean section of this book.

The Mont Fleur Conference Venue is snuggled in mountains among the vineyards of Stellenbosch. It played an honoured part in South Africa's post-apartheid history because it was here that the Mont Fleur Scenario Exercise took place over four weekends in 1992. A broad, multi-racial mix of South

African opinion leaders, drawn from politics, business and civil society, framed four different scenarios for the country in the next decade, ranging from the optimistic 'Flight of the Flamingos' to the pessimistic 'Ostrich', with 'Lame Duck' and 'Icarus' sitting uncomfortably or precariously in the middle. Happily, South Africa's fortunes since 1992 have largely reflected the future imagined in 'Flight of the Flamingos'. Today Mont Fleur provides the setting for the first module of the flagship Tutu Fellowship Leadership Programme (which also encompasses scenario creation) that is organised and facilitated by the African Leadership Institute, of which I am honoured to be a Director and Trustee. 'Regeneration' is set at Mont Fleur and is a very personal and somewhat complex poem. I attempt to elucidate further upon its key facets in the supplementary notes on page 97.

The Pumpkin or the Cow

I parked my car near Barrydale
To start out on my quest,
Found a well-marked mountain trail
And tackled it with zest.

I strolled along with lazy grace,
Weighed what my friends had said,
I needed time and peace and space
To plan the years ahead.

I dwelt upon some well-worn themes,
Forged few things that were new,
Slashed away the wilder dreams,
The path ran straight and true.

Then I came to rocky ground,
My pace dropped to a crawl,
Thoughts were even less profound,
I reached a waterfall.

I slumped to earth a weary man
And all I yearned for now
Was a slice of homemade fruit flan
At the Pumpkin[1] or the Cow[2].

I drank a little from a spring,
Then set off up a slope,
My mind distilled another thing
That gave me future hope.

The trail divided at the top,
My choice the route straight on,
I judged a cherished scheme a flop,
One more illusion gone.

The waymark arrows disappeared
To strand me on a peak,

My addled brain now swiftly cleared,
I scrambled down a creek.

My body took a lot of flak,
I shredded my best shorts,
Large pebbles bruised my aching back,
This stopped all further thoughts.

I rested under cloudless sky
And wondered if somehow
I could have a homemade meat pie
At the Pumpkin or the Cow.

I crossed a tangled, shallow ditch
And came out on some tar,
Then Fate unfurled a further glitch,
I couldn't find my car.

I dragged my wounded, cramping legs
Into dense bush and fern,
A thicket full of barbs and pegs
That thwarted every turn.

Six times I fell into a brook,
Then pulled myself upright,
I suffered pain each step I took
But won this final fight.

Now my journey reached its end
With two key lessons learned,
Courage is your truest friend
And what means most is earned.

Survival, life's one timeless art,
Inspired my joyous vow –
To celebrate with milk tart[3]
At the Pumpkin or the Cow.

---

1 *The Country Pumpkin tearoom in Barrydale*

2 *The Blue Cow tearoom in Barrydale*

3 *A traditional (and delicious!) South African dessert*

INTERLUDE

I thought it quite polite to greet
My neighbour on the rock;
He lay there in the scorching sun,
All curled up in a block.

I moved a step along the path,
Intent to call "Good Day";
My neighbour raised his awesome head
Just fifteen feet away.

He started to uncoil himself,
His movement was so smooth;
I checked the greeting in my throat
And made a backward move.

His length grew greater all the time,
Or so it seemed to me,
His jet black presence held me rapt
And froze me on the scree.

My mind distilled an ancient myth,
The serpent tempting Eve,
For I was drawn towards the snake[1]
And had no wish to leave.

The snake was king in this domain
And he would make the choice -
To send me silent from his hill
Or let me have my voice.

He peered at me through narrowed lids,
His tongue flicked to and fro;
It seemed unlikely we'd be friends;
I judged it best to go.

I scrambled down the slope I'd climbed
And bade the snake farewell;
It was a stirring interlude-
And one more tale to tell.

1 *Cape cobra*

Regeneration*

I slog through fynbos[1]
Up the mountain;
God, it's hard in this heat!
It melts the spirit and burns the brain.
Just put one foot after the other
And watch the path
For snakes.
Mont Fleur[2] lies far below,
White walls gleaming in the sun,
Green lawns,
And talented young leaders
Come to hone their skills
And fuel ambition
To regenerate Africa.
Their trail will be as long and steep
As this -
But they have youth and energy,
While mine have faded
With the stagnant years.
I struggle to the top,
Seeking water,
But the streams are dry as my ambition;
No spring to slake my thirst
For fresh vigour.
I pant back to the refuge of Mont Fleur,
My comfort zone,
Then listen to the dreams
Of those who hope to lead us all
To better times;
Offer safe advice to people seeking wisdom
And the Holy Grail;
So I pass the balance of the day.

The skies darken
With the anger of the gods
At this slice of Africa;
They roar and flash in rage,
Hurl their shards of hail
At arid hills
And my complacency.
A bolt of lightning
Shatters soft illusions,
Thunder hammers loudly
At the tissue of my mind;
Relentless rain
Drowns fragile thoughts;
I fall to fitful sleep.

I waken to the remnants of the storm.
Nascent sun thins cloud,
Lighting up the vineyards
That burst with new sprung growth;
Withered vines shoot green,
Grasses sprout,
And waxbills[3] *swee* the dawning of clear day.
The vibrant sound
Of moisture on the move
Drives me down
A scented path;
Everywhere the surge
Of rippling water,
Cascading from the slopes
And spurting to the sea.
I hug the shimmering sky
In gratitude for life
And reborn zest
To help the young elite.

They'll navigate the streams of hope
That start to flow
Through Africa -
I will add my paddle
To their boat.

* *Supplementary notes on this poem can be found in the Appendix*

---

1 *The natural heath land vegetation in coastal and montane areas of the Western Cape*

2 *Conference Venue at which a module of the Arcbishop Tutu Fellowship Leadership Programme is held*

3 *Small songbirds whose call resembles "swee"; this particular species is known as the swee waxbill*

MADAGASCAN POEMS

Introduction*

Madagascar, the world's fourth largest island, lies in the Indian Ocean a few hundred miles from the African mainland. Very little from the mainland has penetrated, or even infiltrated, there, which is both a delight and a disappointment to me. A delight because virtually everything you see or touch or taste is different, and, in a good many cases, unique and a disappointment because Madagascar almost totally lacks the element of menace that makes journeys to the wilder parts of Africa so stimulating. Madagascar is not altogether without its dangers - the steep, rocky, vine-strewn trails demand extreme care - but, the odd crocodile or scorpion apart, none of its natural inhabitants is equipped to inflict significant harm upon you, not even the myriad snakes, spiders and creepy crawlies. Lions, leopards, cheetahs and even servils would sneer at Madagascar's only mammalian predator, the fossa, which preys upon rotund birds and small lemurs.

The lemurs are an undiluted joy. Eighty or so species have been identified to date (new ones are progressively being discovered in remote parts of the island). The most intriguing of them, as well as being the largest, is the indri; these endearing animals live in small family groups in dense rain forest and communicate through harmonized song with neighbouring families, often a mile or more distant. Predominant among the other mammals are the zebu, ubiquitous hump-backed cattle introduced from India, which are to be found in abundance everywhere outside the protected forest areas.

The above themes and subjects are developed further in the poems 'Madagascar', 'The Indri' and 'Zebu' that follow. 'The Flufftail' records the pursuit of an elusive bird in the magnificent Ranomafana National Park under the expert tutelage of Fidi, one of life's great characters and a veritable 'one-off' among guides. It is a cautionary tale, one that will be familiar to birdwatchers anywhere in the world.

Madagascar is at once a naturalist's deepest bliss and his or her worst nightmare. It has a matchless variety of fauna and flora but 90% of the original acreage of forest (which covered virtually the entire island) has been slashed, burned or otherwise destroyed by man during the span of a few centuries to make temporary way for agriculture, principally to create rice paddies and impoverished pastures for zebu. It is temporary because the land that has been cleared has retreated rapidly into desert. Fortunately, there is now a very active programme to preserve as much as possible of the surviving forest and numerous national parks and special reserves have been established. I describe the rapid environmental decline of the once pristine island in 'The Frigatebird', the mighty flyer of that name being to all appearances a survivor from prehistoric times.

In addition to the despoliation of its landscape, Madagascar witnessed unspeakable violations of human dignity in its darker years. The slave trade flourished there, as I recount in 'Black Rocks'; more detailed notes can be read on pages 97 and 98.

All in all, despite its imperfections, Madagascar is magical and I cannot wait to return there.

* Written just before the present civil strife in the country which will make travel there difficult

MADAGASCAR

You broke from old Gondwanaland[1] and drifted out to sea,
Devised the strangest island life that there could ever be,
Spurning tall savannah grass[2] you sprouted forest-tree,
You're not the drought-torn Africa where death strikes constantly:
You are....
Madagascar!

You culled the violent carnivores that ripped their prey apart,
Filtered out large animals and bid them all depart,
Your gentle lemurs prancing round now melt the hardest heart,
You'll never be harsh Africa where carnage is an art:
You are....
Madagascar!

You once had great birds ten feet tall[3] but they're no longer found,
The species you replaced them with are mainly short and round,
Seldom spreading wing to fly they creep along the ground,
You're not the vibrant Africa where fearsome hawks abound:
You are....
Madagascar!

You had no place for deadly snakes and cast them all aside,
Introduced some harmless herps[4] that only want to hide,
Melting into leaves and bark they might as well have died,
You cannot be the Africa where reptiles prowl with pride:
You are....
Madagascar!

You blew out all volcano smoke a million years ago,
Left a trail of tsingi[5] rock that marked the lava flow,
Nothing gaining access there will find the means to grow;
You still don't boast the killer-scapes that Africa can show:
You are....
Madagascar!

Your people never took to maize however low the price,
Stripped away most forest growth and planted fields of rice,
Seeking flavour for their food they cultivated spice[6],
I wish you could be Africa but you are far too nice:
You are ....
Madagascar!

1 *A huge supercontinent that covered most of the Southern Hemisphere about 200 million years ago*

2 *Tall, bronze grass that grows in much of mainland Africa*

3 *Notably the 'elephant bird' which became extinct at about the same time as the dodo and was reputedly the largest bird known to the modern world*

4 *Vernacular term for reptiles and amphibians, including chameleons, geckos, lizards and snakes*

5 *Sharp-edged limestone, extensive in area, that is difficult to traverse*

6 *Madagascar provides the world with a great variety of spices, including cinnamon, nutmeg and cloves*

The Flufftail

We'd spent the day at 'Fana[1]
With Fidi as our guide,
Scooting up the matted slopes
Then down the other side;
I thought we looked for lemurs,
But that was my mistake,
For Fidi sought a flufftail
As we foundered in his wake.

I've seen a lot of couas[2],
Some rails[3] and vangas[4] too;
But what the hell's a flufftail,
Is it black or brown or blue?

We scrambled into forest,
Through tangled vines and roots,
Ignored the soaring raptors
And lemurs munching shoots;
With Fidi always leading,
His head bent to the ground,
We tried to find a flufftail
(Reluctant to be found).

I've seen some owls and herons,
An oxylabes[5] too;
But what the hell's a flufftail,
Would I know it if it flew?

We stopped at last in silence
As Fidi cupped his hand,
He piped a mournful melody
That echoed through the land;
From deep within the forest
A sombre bird replied,
We'd heard a distant flufftail
And Fidi puffed with pride.

I've seen a mass of fodies[6],
Ground-rollers[7] at nightfall;
But what the hell's a flufftail,
Is it large or squat or small?

The flufftail ventured closer,
Or so friend Fidi said,
To me its call seemed fainter
And I turned away my head;
Fidi dragged me back again,
He leapt high in the air,
His finger started stabbing,
"It's there! It's there! It's there!"

I traced the pointing finger
And looked low in a tree;
Where the hell's the flufftail?
Where can the damn thing be?

Fidi waved his arms about,
His anger was profound,
"The flufftail's right in front of you,
It's walking on the ground!"
He clasped me by the elbow
And pulled me to his side,
But still I couldn't find it,
No matter how I tried.

"Too late! Too late!" screamed Fidi,
"It's disappeared from view";
So what the hell's a flufftail,
Is it brown or black or blue?

---

1 *Ranomafana National Park*

2 *Species of Madagascan bird, most members of which are found nowhere else in the world*

3, 4, 5, 6 *& 7 As above*

THE INDRI[1]

Lead me to the indri, please,
I want to hear them sing;
Guide me up the forest trails
To where they launch their soulful wails
That call to mind the grisly tales
Of harpies[2] on the wing.

Let me stand beneath the trees
And wait for them to move;
They leap from any spindly bough,
Find a spot to land somehow,
Shriek a hearty high-pitched vow
Their timing will improve.

Help me choose the closest place
To view them while they stay;
They look benign as cuddly toys,
Bicker like young girls and boys,
Take delight in simple joys
Of children at their play.

Tell me when they'll have the grace
To burst into their song;
I thought they'd start up by this time,
But all they've done is act in mime,
Perhaps this group is past its prime
Or been awake too long.

Hold me as I crane my head
To watch them climb up high;
A chorus has begun to flower,
It rises with an awesome power
To make the bravest creatures cower
And lesser beings cry.

Keep me here until I'm dead,
This is my greatest prize;
Adult tenors fuel the choir,
Young sopranos drive them higher,
Their voices never seem to tire
And proudly harmonize.

Assure me they'll descend anon,
Those lemurs are so quaint;
I'll tolerate a long delay,
It's still quite early in the day,
They cannot be too far away –
No, their carolling grows faint.

Console me now they've been and gone,
It is the saddest thing;
I fell in love right from the start,
Those gorgeous creatures stole my heart,
But now the time has come to part;
I've heard the indri sing.

---

1 *Largest of the living lemurs*

2 *In Greek and Roman mythology, these were monsters with a woman's head and body and a bird's wings and claws*

Zebu[1]

Zebu! A name so redolent of power,
Indians would regard them as divine,
Here in Madagascar they constitute the dower,
A measure of your wealth compared to mine.

Zebu! They might be riches to a man,
It's such a shame they look like dowdy lumps,
Some of them are brindle, others of them tan,
With, on their backs, extraordinary humps.

Zebu! You find them all across the land,
Forests have been cleared to let them graze,
The pasture lacks nutrition, much of it is sand,
How sad it is they cannot feed on maize.

Zebu! They're scrawny but so strong,
They pull a cart or plough without a break;
With all that mighty effort they do not last for long
And end up in a pot as stewing steak.

1 *Hump-backed cattle that are also found in number in India*

BLACK ROCKS*

You rest within the forest in a quiet and sheltered place,
Buttressed by large rocks from wind and rain;
You earned the lasting comfort of your coffin's close embrace,
A martyr while you breathed to stress and pain.

Who brought you to these sandy shores two hundred years ago?
It could have been French pirates or the Dutch;
What distant land they stole you from the world will never know,
Or who it was that loved you and how much.

You came to Nosy Mangabe[1] as one of many slaves,
Some due to be transported far away;
The others were denied the chance to die among the waves,
Condemned by man's cruel hand to timeless stay.

You would have cut down massive trees and hauled them to the ships,
The source of untold wealth to those you served;
They broke your fragile courage using rustic flails and whips,
Contrived to keep you thoroughly unnerved.

Your manly strength sustained you till you had no more to give,
Then some disease provoked your liberty;
There is no record left to us of when you ceased to live,
The smallest hint of what your name might be.

Your fellow slaves who mourned you put your body in a pit,
Where they were laid beside you in their turn;
When more enlightened men arrived, the skeletons were split,
Revered as missing ancestors, we learn.

They placed you in a coffin which they dragged far up a trail,
Until you reached an outcrop called Black Rocks;
Some men with flags broke into song and girls knelt low to wail,
Your coffin was secured on granite blocks.

I came across that coffin as I trudged up Mangabe
In vain pursuit of aye-aye[2] gnawing bark;
My torch revealed a modest board that told me where you lay -
I paid my silent homage in the dark.

Although you died in slavery your spirit wanders free,
It touched me as I hurtled down a vine;
For while my five companions said my saviour was a tree,
I'm sure your ghostly hand was grasping mine.

THE FRIGATEBIRD[1]

How many worlds have you explored,
Then gauged what each was worth?
You might have glimpsed Gondwanaland[2]
Or Africa's new birth,
A time when pterodactyls[3] flew,
When mammoths[4] strode the Earth.

Within the late Cretaceous age[5]
This island's day first dawned;
You must have flown in virgin sky
To view the life it spawned,
Fresh forest bursting through the rock,
Most lush but some parts thorned.

What ancient marvels did you see
When soaring past this coast?
Of all our Eocene[6] ancestors
Which one impressed you most?
Perhaps old Daubentonia[7],
The aye-aye's[8] giant ghost.

You watched the treescape evanesce
Soon after man arrived,
The forest growth was slashed and burned
And nothing large survived,
The smaller remnants struggled on
But mostly ducked and dived.

And now you check my every move
Upon this coral beach;
I gaze up at your silhouette
So far beyond my reach;
What wisdom I could draw from you
If you had power to teach.

You lived through all the aeons spent
In fashioning this land;
Now in the blinking of Time's eye
You find it stripped to sand;
What message do you have for us
That we will understand?

---

1 *An enormous piratical seabird which looks like a relic from our prehistoric past*

2 *A huge supercontinent that covered most of the Southern Hemisphere about 200 million years ago*

3 *Winged dinosaurs*

4 *Ancient ancestors of the elephant*

5 *A period of geological time approximately 143 to 65 million years ago*

6 *The Eocene epoch lasted from about 55 to 34 million years ago*

7 *An extinct species of aye-aye, about five times larger than the present animal; it survived until about 1220 AD*

8 *The largest nocturnal lemur; it is undoubtedly one of the wierdest looking creatures on the planet*

MISCELLANEOUS POEMS

Introduction

I have written very few poems that have no connection whatsoever with Africa and most of those do not merit reproduction. Each of the two that I am including in this book centres upon an individual with whom I never conversed but who nevertheless made a deep and lasting impact upon me.

I have been fortunate enough to enjoy a varied and interesting life and am frequently asked to identify the person who has most impressed me. My answer is consistent and never fails to astonish. It is someone who swept the pavements outside Buckingham Palace, which I walked past for many years on my way to work in Piccadilly from Victoria station. The sweeper was an elderly man who seemed utterly at peace with himself and his environment, oblivious to the throng of tourists who gawped through the Palace railings, and the trusted friend of every bird within earshot. When he emitted a gentle whistle a miscellany of birds flew in from every direction and settled upon his arms and bowed back. Never before or since have I encountered anybody with that degree of affinity to nature. My tribute to him is contained in 'Communion'.

How often does one travel on a train or bus and sit next to or opposite someone for a significant period without learning (or wanting to learn) the first thing about him or her? The answer is probably in about 99.9% of instances. That is certainly my experience. In 'Brief Encounter' I describe the exceptional situation. Regrettably, I have never 'met' the woman in question again as she fascinated me and probably had a compelling story to tell.

The final poem is 'Africa Revisited', which I originally wrote on a postcard that I sent from Kenya to a friend in England. As much as my heart lies in Africa and as much as I might dream about living there again, I would miss large elements of my present life in England - the variable weather (surprisingly!), the different seasons, especially the winter, the moors and the Downs, the wonderful Thames and, most of all, my family and friends. I want to continue to visit different parts of Africa for as long as humanly possible but my days of residing there are past. This takes me rather neatly back to 'The African Sun' at the beginning of this book and to my failure in my advancing years to unleash the blood red ball lodged firmly in my childhood eye.

COMMUNION

He stoops and finds God on the pavement,
Among the dutiful feet
That trudge towards the Palace[1],
In tired pursuit of splendour.
His hand-hewn brush dispels a clod
That might offend the welling herd,
As he hums a simple tune of
Invitation to his friends.

His wealth transcends all other in that crowd,
For he is Nature's serf and king,
An ancient child untouched by care of time,
Whose soul communes with the distant sky,
With the smallest bird on the humblest tree.
He holds his world in a gnarled brown hand,
A trusted palm where sparrows lightly fuss
And bid spry welcome to a reverential thrush,
Who trills in unashamed delight
A hymn of praise upon the altar
Of the old man's cambered back.

Some languid doves swell the throng
Of worshippers and worshipped,
And feed upon the greying crusts
The veteran draws from dusty pockets;
No shallow words spoil
The silent bond of Nature with this man,
As he bends once more to chat with God.

---

1 *Buckingham Palace in London*

BRIEF ENCOUNTER

We met on the tube[1]
At Baker Street[2];
Eight o'clock.
You sat next to me
Or I sat next to you,
No matter which.
You wore a stylish skirt
And diamond ring;
Hair cut short,
With fringe,
No lustre.
You never looked at me
But I saw you;
Dismay
Etched in your face,
Not pretty,
Yet still a bit
Attractive.
Fingers clenched,
Clasping bag,
Staring into space;
You pinched your lip,
Sucked your thumb
Like a child;
But what child looks
So tired and drawn,
And full of sorrow?
You closed your eyes,
Heavy lids,
Shadowed,
Lined with worry;
Scratched your nose
And sighed;

A pensive sound
That only we could hear.
You chewed your nails,
Twice,
Rubbed your upper lip,
Cupped your chin
In your hand.
What troubled you:
Man or job
Or debt
Or life itself?
I cared but never knew;
You never knew I cared.
We exited at Charing Cross[3]
At eight ten.
You first,
Then me behind,
Shared the escalator
To the top;
You left me.

---

1 *The vernacular name for a train on the London Underground system*

2 *A station on the London Underground*

3 *Another station on the London Underground*

Africa Revisited

The harsh sun bakes my addled mind
And burns away my childhood dream
To venture far to Europe
And beyond.
That dream is long fulfilled -
But I am unfulfilled.

Now I yearn for Africa again;
Parched hills and plains,
Squat trees,
And multitudes of animals and birds
Too numerous
For anyone to name;
BUT.....
I would sorely miss
My friends like you!

Appendix

Supplementary Notes on Selected Poems

Notes on the Elephants Trilogy

I have had many wonderful trips into the African bush, particularly in Zimbabwe, and there are numerous incidents involving a variety of animals about which I might have written poems. But, for the time being at least, the 'bush poems' are limited to 'First Love', 'The Silence of the Veldt' and the Elephants trilogy - 'Elephants', 'More Elephants' and 'Elephants Again'. That I have focused on elephants is readily explained. Of all the magnificent animals in Africa, they are my clear favourite; physically imposing and constantly compelling attention and respect, yet surprisingly tolerant of, and gentle towards, humans when they do not feel threatened.

Each tale in the trilogy is true in the smallest detail yet I can honestly attest that never once was I unduly concerned by the proximity of the elephants I describe, whether it be while I was dozing on the ground, sluicing my canoe in the water or pushing my way through an assembly of young bulls to my sleeping accommodation. Although it seems scarcely credible, on each occasion the elephants arrived unnoticed; when they choose to they can move so quietly that you do not hear them.

The nocturnal escapade related in 'Elephants' took place at an upland camp (formerly a private hunting lodge) located in a remote part of the Hwange National Park, just south of the Victoria Falls. The various incidents referred to in 'More Elephants' all occurred during an extended trek in the Chizarira gorges in search of taita falcons. The encounter in 'Elephants Again' occupied a few memorable minutes of a canoe safari along the Zambezi River in the vicinity of the Mana Pools Reserve.

Notes on 'The Angry Child'

'The Angry Child' is set in 1990, when all seemed serene and progressive in Zimbabwe to the external gaze. Indeed, in those now distant days, Zimbabwe was to many the shining example of how an African country could flourish under its new, post-colonial rulers.

However, beneath the apparently calm surface, there were still tensions between the Mashona people, the majority ethnic group in Zimbabwe, with their centre in Harare, and the Matabele, the minority ethnic group, centred in Bulawayo. There had always been tribal jealousies, even during the 'war of liberation' during the 1970s, but these intensified after independence in 1980 when the Matabele sensed they were being shortchanged and a number of dissident groups became active, the most prominent being one led by Lookout Masuku. In an effort to stamp out the potential insurrection, Prime Minister Robert Mugabe sent in the Fifth Brigade, troops who had been specially trained in counter insurgency techniques by North Korean 'advisers'. The Fifth Brigade did eventually quell the dissidents but only after there had been large scale massacres of the Matabele. This received very little coverage in the press either within or outside Zimbabwe although some courageous reporters did try to bring the situation to the attention of the world. Notable among them was Peter Godwin, who subsequently wrote 'Mukiwa' and who has recently produced 'When a Crocodile eats the Sun'. In 'Mukiwa', he gives graphic details of the incidents in Matabeleland, including the discovery of countless bodies hurled into mineshafts. His reward for his honest and courageous reporting was to be declared an enemy of the State and he was forced to leave Zimbabwe. In Mashonaland, there has always been a refusal, or, at the very least, a reluctance, to acknowledge that anything untoward happened in Matabeleland in the 1980s and reports of the massacre were dismissed as propaganda disseminated by enemies of Zimbabwe.

The analysis of personality for business leadership purposes is very much in vogue nowadays. We are all apparently an amalgam of 'child', 'parent' and 'adult', with the first two establishing our emotions and the latter introducing a moderating element into our thoughts and actions. The 'child' can be angry or happy or withdrawn and the 'parent' can be strict or caring. The 'adult' does not have emotions that are independent from the 'child' or 'parent' and is entirely rational. Some young Africans who participated in a Leadership Workshop that I attended in South Africa *(see notes on 'Regeneration' on page 97)* were assessed by experts in terms of 'angry child' or 'withdrawn child' or 'natural child' or 'strict parent' or 'nurturing parent' or 'adult'. The individual who was most obviously an 'angry child' was a Matabele in his early thirties. He did not care for this description much but, after a pause or two for reflection, accepted that it was perhaps accurate and he then explained why this was so. His story is distilled in my poem, although some details have been changed, and the dialogue between teacher and student is entirely of my own invention.

Notes on 'The Doctor's Dilemma'

'The Doctor's Dilemma' is a fictional tale about the stark choices that confront medical practitioners in allocating extremely scarce drugs among an avalanche of patients in the present-day Zimbabwe. It is, however, inspired by a true story related by another of the young Africans participating in the Leadership Workshop referred to above. She was a doctor practising at a major hospital in Harare (which I believe has since closed) and had to decide to which of two patients she should prescribe a meagre quantity of tablets that might help to keep them alive for a little longer. There was probably no wrong or right choice in this instance as each of the patients had a legitimate claim to be treated, but she was troubled by the one she ultimately made after much agonising. By favouring one patient over the other for what were, in essence, 'pragmatic reasons' (the nature of which I will not divulge), she was concerned that she might have acted unethically - the topic being discussed during this segment of the Workshop was 'ethical leadership'. All those listening leapt to her defence as they detected no hint of immorality in her behaviour but her story brought home all too forcibly to the audience the stark reality of life in Zimbabwe and the awesome challenges faced by the many excellent people who are still striving to improve the quality of life of their fellow citizens. I should emphasise that the dilemma in the true story is not one of those that the doctor in my poem had to address.

Notes on 'Ubuntu'

There is a considerable literature on the subject of ubuntu, the heart-warming tradition that has historically served as the cornerstone of society in the southern part of Africa.

I have seen the term 'ubuntu' translated as "I am because we are: I can only be a person through others". It defines the individual in terms of his or her relationship with others. According to this definition, individuals only exist in their relationships with others and, as those relationships change, so do the characters of the individuals. There is thus an interdependence that underpins all African society.

Archbishop Desmond Tutu has said of ubuntu: "It is about the essence of being human. We believe that a person is a person through other persons: that my humanity is bound up and caught up in yours. When I dehumanise you, I inexorably dehumanise myself. The solitary human being is a contradiction in terms and therefore you seek to work for the common good because your humanity comes into its own in community, in belonging."

Furthermore, the concept of 'I am because we are' extends both to one's forbears and to one's successors. My humanity has its genesis in those who came before me, to whom I must pay due homage (ancestor worship), and will be my legacy to those who come after me, which legacy I must protect. Hence I am my forbear and I am my successor and they are me. I believe that Buddhists have a very similar philosophy.

I hope that the above snippets have not made what constitutes ubuntu more opaque to the reader than it was before! They do, perhaps, lend some force to the cynics who believe that ubuntu is largely 'smoke and mirrors', particularly when one witnesses the ruinous state of countries like Zimbabwe (which was at the forefront of my mind when I wrote the poem). I am not a cynic and firmly believe that ubuntu will endure and that it will freshly inspire a more enlightened future generation of African leaders.

'Ubuntu' is one of only four poems in this book to have been 'published' in some manner before, the others being 'The Distant Drums', 'The Pumpkin or the Cow' and 'Closure'.

Notes on 'The Birthday Party'

'The Birthday Party' was engendered by a short newsreel on BBC television about the celebration near Beit Bridge (on the arid Limpopo River that marks Zimbabwe's border with South Africa) of the 84th birthday of President Robert Mugabe. If anything could chill one's blood and cause one's hackles to rise at the same time, this was definitely it! The pictures showed the President in a flowing shirt adorned by his own image; hundreds of his acolytes were similarly attired. The choice of clothing of the acolytes was perhaps understandable but for Mugabe to feel the need to gaze down on his own face is surely the ultimate manifestation of megalomania.

This exercise in extreme self-indulgence seemed to be primarily designed to taunt a group of Zimbabwean refugees gathered on the South African side of the barbed wire with the inviolability of Mugabe and his brutal regime; the images will remain forever imprinted on my mind.

I have used a measure of poetic licence in 'The Birthday Party'. I did not witness the details of the feast but do not think it is stretching credibility too far to imagine that at least some of the food consumed was either 'contributed' by impoverished subsistence farmers in the area or removed from stocks earmarked by aid agencies for the alleviation of starvation (I have read various reports about the privileged minority routinely purloining donated items for their own base purposes). Everything else I describe was only too horribly real!

Robert Mugabe, as entrenched in power as ever, notwithstanding the ostensible division of ministerial responsibilities with Morgan Tsvangirai, has recently enjoyed his 85th birthday, which, it was well publicized, featured the consumption of large quantities of lobsters and champagne. All this in a land where most of the people are starving.

Notes on 'Regeneration'

This poem describes regeneration on three levels - the reinvigoration of the parched hills and vineyards adjoining the Mont Fleur Conference Venue near Stellenbosch in South Africa; the potential renaissance of Africa envisaged by the group of young leaders participating in a Leadership Workshop at Mont Fleur *(about which, more below)*; and my own transformation from a somewhat detached onlooker at the Workshop to someone firmly committed to assisting those leaders (and the participants in future programmes run by the African Leadership Institute) in whatever small measure I can.

The underlying philosophy of the African Leadership Institute, a charitable body which has Archbishop Desmond Tutu as its Patron and of which I am a Director and Trustee, is that good leadership in all sectors of society is vital for the future success of Africa. It has targeted the next generation of Africa's leaders (in the 25 to 39 age group) with the objective of nurturing the leadership capabilities of the cream of this group, building a pan-African network of those individuals, and encouraging them to apply their leadership capabilities for the betterment of the greater community.

The Institute's flagship project is the Archbishop Tutu Fellowship Leadership Programme, which is run in partnership with the Said Business School of Oxford University, African institutions and commercial sponsors. The object of the Programme is to provide a select group of twenty high potential leaders with an intensive learning and broadening experience on the principles and application of leadership, with particular emphasis on African leadership in a global context, and with the confidence, experiences, tools and insights to enable them to be effective both in Africa and in the global arena. The participants (who become Tutu Fellows if they complete the Programme to the Institute's satisfaction) are drawn from across Africa and from various sectors, ranging from business to civil society. They are selected on merit without regard to ethnicity or gender.

More about the Institute and its activities can be found at: *www.alinstitute.org.*

Notes on 'Black Rocks'

Madagascar is a country that was tarnished by the slave trade. I must confess that this is a subject about which I knew very little until a visit to the beautiful island of Nosy Mangabe in the north east of the country provoked a strong interest. The object of that visit was to find the aye-aye, the largest of the nocturnal lemurs and one of the strangest creatures on Earth. A decade ago the species was feared to be virtually extinct, Nosy Mangabe being one of its few remaining 'strongholds', but recent evidence suggests that it is distributed more widely throughout Madagascar than originally thought and its numbers may be reasonably healthy.

The references in 'Black Rocks' to the treatment of slaves while they were alive, their consignment to pits on death and the reverent reburial of their skeletons by more enlightened generations in the latter part of the nineteenth century are based on the factual research that I conducted upon my return to London. However, what inspired me to write the poem was the experience of sitting beside a slave's simple coffin at a small cemetery (Black Rocks) high in the hills of Nosy Mangabe towards the top of a steep, rugged and root-ridden trail. I wondered, in particular, where the slave might originally have come from, who his loved ones might have been and why he was left to work and die in Nosy Mangabe, rather than being transported to some distant land.

Later the same day, after a fruitless search for the aye-aye in pitch darkness (I subsequently saw the animal elsewhere in Madagascar), my companions and I arrived at Black Rocks again. About fifty yards beyond this spot I nearly came to grief when I placed my right foot on what seemed to be a solid rock at the edge of the trail and it broke away, causing me to lurch sideways. I uttered a cry like Tarzan and, in falling, managed to grab a long lianna (vine) which mercifully held my weight as I swung around and located terra firma again. There was a twenty foot drop beneath me while I was airborne. I would like to think that it was the friendly spirit of the slave that guided my hand to the vine and ensured it was strong enough to support me!